# Sacred Fool

# Sacred Fool

## The Fantastic Adventures of
## Alejandro Jodorowsky
## (A Love Letter)

Nathan Dean Talamantez

atmosphere press

**Dear Jodo,**

I wonder what it was about your first feature-length film, *Fando Y Lis*, that provoked an angry mob to seek your life on that hot night in Acapulco. Was it the film's nudity? Its violence? Or was it the psychological pain Fando inflicted upon Lis? Indeed, if all the film's action occurred within the couple's short journey to the fabled city of Tar, then Lis' devotion to Fando appears absurd. But the way I interpreted the film, each atrocity was separated by the numbing agent of years, allowing time to obscure Lis' tragedy and eventual murder from herself.

I decided to write a story about you in a similar manner: a lifetime of adventures portrayed within a few short years. After all, Jodo, you are very old. I cannot pack eighty years of artistic exploits into one tale without using some reductive techniques. So, consider my work a creative reimagining, like your adaption of the story of the Mexican serial killer Goyo Cardenas in *Santa Sangre*.

You are undoubtedly asking yourself why I am writing a story to tell you about your own life. It is because I love you; because your art has meant the world to me, and this is the gift I can give in return. It is the same one you gave me: a view of yourself twisted through a prism by which I may show you something about yourself you've never seen before. Or perhaps I am primarily speaking to myself. But, like the game of telephone, I will tell you what you whispered to me so you can hear it too.

We begin in Tocopilla, Chile, that most unhappy time. Of course, isolation can develop into powerful creativity, but at the time, all we felt was loneliness. When I was growing up in San Antonio, Texas, my parents' hyper-religious lifestyle made me uncomfortable around other children. There was one reality the rest of the world operated in, and another, more severe one waiting at home. To help, I have given you magical eyes. You already had them, but now they will have physical dimensions.

I read that your family's status as immigrants made you feel like an outcast as well. Biographies always refer to you as a French-Chilean filmmaker, though to my knowledge, you share no biological heritage with either; but are of Russian/Jewish descent. And then, you chose to make most of your films in Mexico, practically adopting it, calling it a land of magic. I ask you, Alejandro, what are you? Is any aspect of your being tied to a national identity?

Being mixed-blood, even after serving in the military, I never developed a strong sense of ethnic or national heritage. So, without roots, how did we grow? Wild. That is why, in my story, I provided you with a mentor—someone like Theosophist in *La Danza de la Realidad* mixed with Friedrich Nietzsche's eternally reoccurring Übermensch. But Apollonius will teach you to develop your powers.

*"You are the eternal witness. The drop of water that will never become one with the great ocean."*

*-The Incal*

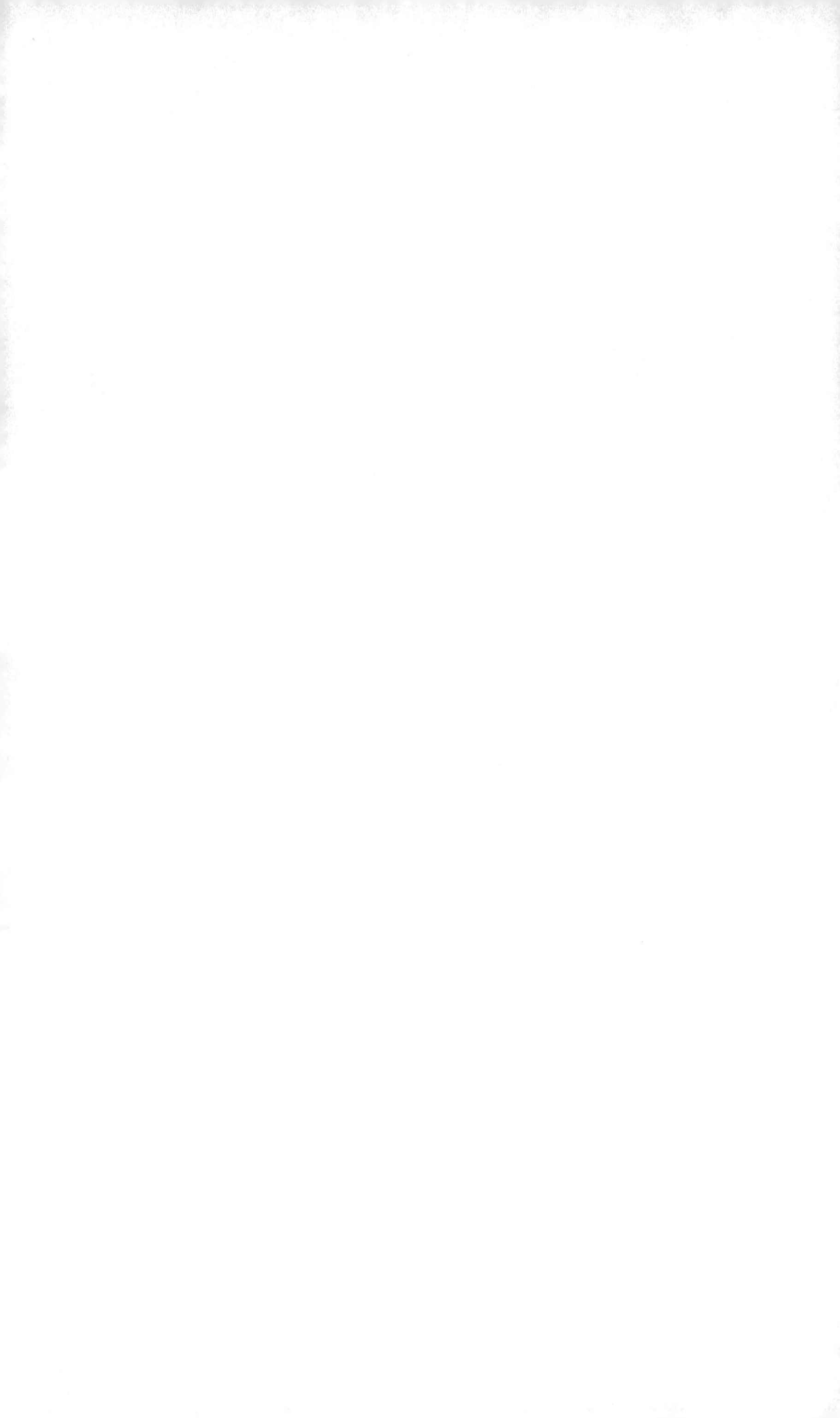

# Chapter 1:
## The Boy with Magic Eyes

The moment a baby is born, if it cries, it is best to sit it upright, grasp one of its tiny paws, and welcome it properly to this planet. This will help orient it. Otherwise, if the world proves dangerous and full of monsters, the infant may reject its reality altogether. It will turn its head, cross its eyes, and wail for its lost paradise. If this happens, take comfort. If you are the type of parent who cares enough to worry about these things, then hug your child, and it will more than likely turn out fine. But, if the initial trauma of birth goes unresolved, and the child grows without ever finding comfort or safety, then its equilibrium will never properly develop. This is very dangerous. Without a baseline, the child may never learn to unscrew its eyes and operate in the communally shared reality. It will never dance; instead, it will grow to develop vertigo and become unable to tell the difference between this dimension and the next.

Such was the case of young Alejandro Jodorowsky, born in 1929, in a small coastal village in Northern Chile named Tocopilla. He was born to a silent, servile mother, and a father who had even less tolerance for eccentricities than he had affection for his family. Indeed, Alejandro's father was so critical that the boy grew up too afraid to speak, paralyzed by fear. And it was assumed he was mute.

Until age six, Alejandro's vertigo prevented him from learning to walk. And as if his fate wasn't cruel enough, his inability to focus left him with two wandering eyes, rendering him the laughingstock of his peers at school. But with time, and a very pricey specialist his father hired, Alejandro was able to train one eye to remain focused. With one working eye, he could travel to and from the market to purchase groceries for his mother and wander anywhere else where there was an unbroken line of vertical walls he could lean against.

His schoolmates were not sympathetic. They treated him like a monster. Anytime they noticed him hobbling home from the market, holding the wall and carrying his tattered satchel of groceries, they would push him to the ground and steal his fruit, knowing he could not give chase. Because Alejandro's grandparents had emigrated to Chile from Russia, they would also tease him by calling him a foreigner and accusing him of being a Stalinist spy.

In that time, being different was considered a weakness, an intolerable danger to the herd. Because of this logic, in all his village, Alejandro could not make one friend. The only social contact he ever received was from the occasional strangers who had heard stories about him. When they approached, Alejandro already knew what they would ask: about the time in church when mid-ceremony, he flung himself to the ground, then, with a chipped tooth, began screaming as if attacked by a phantom. Or the time he'd levitated while appearing to drown in the middle of the street, then collapsed. "Did he really cough up seawater when he was resuscitated?" they would ask. But under the guise of being mute, Alejandro did not need to answer.

Also, his hunched form, wandering eyes, and lumbering gate inspired many creepy local campfire tales. And it was true; he was a night owl. He would hobble the streets at night with a visage like a goblin, trying to find the best view of the moon. The fishing docks were his favorite. There was an energy there, wild and foreign; sometimes, it created a nearly visible shimmer on the air. He felt it there and in a few other unassuming places, and this was the honey that fed and refreshed Alejandro's soul. In the market, playing children would sing:

*"Will I marry rich, or young, will I die? Alejandro, what do you see out of your right eye?"*

As if he were some type of fortune teller. But was he? What did he see? Many things, and sometimes nothing. Trying to focus on the visions in his right eye felt like falling through floor-after-floor of an interdimensional building or trying to listen to a broadcast with a radio that keeps changing stations. He could not put words to the experience, and this seemed an excellent reason never to speak. If he never spoke, he'd never need to explain himself.

What exists in a world without words?

Plenty, he found.

Movement.

Alejandro could convey everything he ever needed to say through gestures. One day, a well-meaning local artist came into Alejandro's father's linen store to buy material to repair his costume. Wordlessly, through gesture alone, he and Alejandro found much in common and had such a seamless exchange that the artist became possessed by the idea that he must convince Alejandro's father that the boy had a special skill. "He should learn to juggle and become a clown," the artist suggested. But Alejandro's father took this as an insult and became furious, shouting, "No

Jodorowsky will ever become something so foolish as a clown!" Then he punched the poor man in the chin so hard that he came out of one of his shoes.

"How dare he?" Alejandro's father brooded afterward. Besides, his son's future was already planned for him. Alejandro would grow to run and eventually inherit the linen store. And yet, something wasn't working; the boy was failing to meet expectations. So, he decided to remove Alejandro from school, citing that geometry and geography were inconsequential to the practice of running the family's store.

At the quaint boutique, Alejandro got along well enough. He could restock shelves, fold linens, run the cash register with some proficiency, and pen the entire Communist Manifesto from memory—a requirement his father had imposed upon him without the least sense of irony. See, Alejandro's father had the fervent conviction that the revolution was coming; the tyrant Ibanez would be overthrown, and when the classes were equal and the deck reshuffled, the people would realize his greatness and pronounce him King of Chile. Or such went the fantasy.

This was Alejandro's life, and it was meant to be enough.

When he was not busy tending the store, he could be found underneath the fishing pier on the beach; typically, right before sunset wearing his father's UV-protected sunglasses. Twilight was when he received his clearest signal. Right at the moment the sun disappeared on the horizon, there would be a green flash, and data would pulse and flood the air. It was like needles of pleasure piercing every cell of his body. It was overwhelming, overtaking, overpowering euphoria; euphoria that only lasted an instant then left him hungry, starved for another twenty-four hours. The sound of everything in harmony at once, the green flash was the siren, the spark that inspired Alejandro to begin writing poetry. Though not yet with words, within his rich interior, art was being made, nonetheless.

One day, after watching the green flash, with his magic retinas freshly charged, enhancing the fine details of his surroundings, Alejandro noticed several lingering shimmers dancing on the air that somewhat resembled flecks of gold. The tendrils nearest to him were separated by several feet, but as he gazed down the coastline, he noticed they grew closer to each other in proximity.

Alejandro decided to follow the trail.

Eventually, he came to a place where the ocean met the hillside. And still, the flecks continued onward across the sea, hugging the rocky coast.

He meandered but a moment to consider the depth of the water, which only measured halfway up his calves. Then Alejandro rolled up his pantlegs and plunged in. Next came a deeper chill, when Alejandro learned what all adults know, and no child realizes, that the depth of the water continues to rise as you march into the sea. Soon Alejandro was chest-deep looking onward, taking stock of his remaining strength. He continued.

Later he was a rat, with just his head bobbing above the water praying for a miracle; and indeed, there it was, an inlet, a mouth with no more than a twelve-foot beach with dark mud-like sand. He clambered on his knees ashore, where he stripped his clothes and gratefully heaved the night air. Eventually, rising to his feet, he took stock of the wooded canyon before him that opened to the beach through a small trickling stream, and a dense trail of golden particles.

Alejandro had found his path. He walked into the mouth of the verdant fern-covered gully walled by red hills with slopes riddled with snake holes. His shins bled from thorns. He walked for only a few minutes before discovering the ditch dead-ended into a cave. This was not a welcoming cave with a grand chiseled entrance, but rather, the type an eight-year-old boy must stoop to his waist to enter. Alejandro, being a thin-boned but tall teenager, had to crawl. As he entered, his hair was swept back by an overhead mop of grass, causing dust to shower down on him. The dirt mixed with the seawater on his body and solidified, coating him like new skin.

Once inside the cave, gold no longer hung in the air but sat pooled in solid stones the size of grapefruits engrained in the red dirt walls. He considered how a single stone could buy his father a mansion, retirement, whatever was keeping him from being happy. Whatever it took to repurchase Alejandro's life from his parents, it was here in these walls.

The gold glowed with an otherworldly incandescent green, but he assumed it could be traded in the market all the same. He found a sharp rock and began to chip away at the dirt around a large stone, when a voice, as if spoken by the cave itself, boomed forth so powerfully it shook the walls, and they threatened to collapse.

"I don't believe that piece of gold will be nearly as precious to you once you've brought the cave down upon your head. Indeed, this treasure is likely worth much less than you think," the voice said.

Alejandro spun on the voice, pointing a blunt stone

defensively. The beast was like a wall. To his horror, it was stout, hairy like a yeti, and it had wedged itself between the cave's puckered lips and the free night air beyond. Alejandro's knees began to knock, and he would have pissed himself, had his father not appeared in his head, and shouted, "You are a Jodorowsky! Jodorowskys do not piss themselves in battle! Now quickly, go kill this man!" And while Alejandro's mental strain greatened, his back and bearing straightened, then, catlike, he slunk into a low defensive posture.

"Brave lad, but foolish," the towering shadow bellowed. "To seek me out and challenge me in my own home. I may be old..." he sighed heavily, "...but let us see which of us is truly immortal." Then blazes of golden light like a welding torch ignited from the ends of his fingertips. And he slowly raised his hands, taking careful aim.

Watching the unnaturally intricate dance of the flames, Alejandro lost his fear and became entranced. The flames were richly textured, somehow pure, yet not innocent. And from the locks on that internal place that Alejandro had previously identified as shame, escaped three rogue syllables—"Immortal?"

Then, by the magic of his first words, to the beast, Alejandro's innocence became apparent. He snapped, and all but the flame on his index finger doused. Holding this finger ahead of him as a torch, the creature walked toward Alejandro, and what had appeared to be a horrifying beast, instead became a filthy man. He looked wild and flea-infested. It had been long since he had shaved, or bathed, or even dusted for that matter. Clumps of cave hung in caked, dense strands amongst his black mane.

Next, the hermit reassumed a measure of his previous

hostility, rasping out in rapid succession, "Why have you come here? How did you find me?"

For Alejandro, the answers were one. He shyly bent an index finger. Pointing at the air above his head, he said, "The gold. I followed the gold in the air."

The revelation startled the crusty man, who snapped, "No mortal or immortal was ever meant to be able to track me here." He paused contemplatively, then scrambled over to a refuse pile in a weedy corner of the cave's lip. After rifling for a while, he withdrew an aerosol canister and began generously applying it to the air around the cave's perimeter.

"Least of all, a child," he snorted. Then a thought came to him. "Are either of your parents gods?"

Alejandro shrugged.

"Has anyone ever cursed you—or your parents?"

Alejandro shrugged again.

Next, the hermit decided to study the boy. Reaching, from what appeared from Alejandro's perspective to be an unnatural distance, the man latched his fingers on either side of his head and pulled him closer for examination. Then, with his thumbs, the vagrant peeled back Alejandro's eyelids and announced, "Aha! I knew there was something different about you. Your eye is misshapen. It has twisted into a light-bending prism like a conch shell that is made of mirrors."

"A prism?" Alejandro repeated.

"Yes. It's like having a radio that intercepts broadcasts from other dimensions. You can tune in and watch any show you would like. That is how you found me. You followed my sub-human spectrum bioluminescence to my hideaway. See, I, too, was on that pier to observe the green flash and review the information in its data pulse. At sunset, every cough, everyone who died, every deed good and bad gets transferred elsewhere in a mass data dump we call the green flash. It is beautiful, no? You would have never noticed me watching it because I travel too quickly for the villagers to see and do not linger."

"Why?"

"Well, I shouldn't like to be crucified again. I cannot simply go to town. I am Apollonius; my very existence is heresy. For a time, I was nearly indistinguishable from Christ. To be so close, but yet, slightly different, is considered an unforgivable mockery. Alas, I am despised." He looked at his feet sullenly and sniffled a little. "And the tragedy is, I'm not even that guy anymore. I do not want to save humanity anymore. I only want to be normal."

And with that, the burly lump plopped down on a log. His long whiskers melted off his chin, and though his mane remained sodden as ever, his face became like that of an infant, and he began to weep bitterly.

Alejandro, feeling pity for the wretch, sat beside him silently for a time before offering, "Yes, yes, yes, but normality is not being like everyone else. Normality is to be different. Every person is a different person, and one day, you need to be aware of your difference. Aware that you are not the same as others. That is to be normal."

Then, after a few more sniffles, Apollonius ceased to weep. He looked startled and began to age rapidly until he had returned to his previous state. With a look of both confusion and worry, he said, "Oh, that's right. I knew that, once. I must have just ... forgotten." Then he snapped his fingers, and his lucidity instantly returned. "Yes, that's right. You are the one sent to kill me," he said.

Alejandro dropped his protective stone and clasped his hands innocently behind his back.

"No ... Yes. I remember now. It is settled. You will kill me."

"I will not," the boy protested.

"Not now, of course, petulant, impatient youth. I should like to teach you a few lessons first, if it's all the same to you." The elderly man had a limp like Alejandro's. He walked into the cave, directly through Jodorowsky's corporeal form, and rounded a knee-high corner while standing fully upright.

Alejandro pressed and wriggled like an earthworm to follow, hoping not to eventually find his arms pinned and himself trapped to die, having hallucinated the yeti-man after swallowing too much seawater. He could not fathom by what magic the stout hermit had traversed these tight passages.

Finally, on his belly, Alejandro eventually emerged into a sizeable glistening chamber. When he stood, he realized the hall was relatively large, possibly more extensive than his father's store. And it was piled high with more of that eerily incandescent glowing gold. Gold was stacked in bars and coins of every pressing. Some were pressed into similar-sized bricks, while others were incongruous, as if freshly birthed from the calcite deposits themself. Gold made up the cavern's floor. It was pressed in slanted mountains against the walls and met at a low point in the center.

The stranger sat facing away from Alejandro at an austere workbench. As if uninterested, he called behind him:

"First, I will craft another prism to overlay on top of

your own that will allow you to focus. The prism will not heal your vertigo completely, but it will help. Then, once you have adjusted, I will teach you to use the angles of the prism to reveal the unseen. Then, I will teach you to project your own light. Eventually, you will be capable of crafting first-rate illusions by bending it. Finally, should you develop a taste for it, I can teach you to bend reality itself. But be warned, rearranging reality is a dangerous practice that typically unweaves more than it mends. However, that is your lesson to learn; I only provide the means. And in exchange, one day, you will do me this one favor."

The boy never verbally agreed to the pact. But, with a dismissive wave, it seemed apparent that Apollonius considered the matter resolved. The rotund bearlike man remained stooped behind his draftsman's desk, busily walking his compass across a dusty set of schematics. He was now wearing a thicker, tackier set of reading glasses than Alejandro had ever imagined a god would wear. Over his shoulder, Apollonius called, "Go home, for now, boy. But return tomorrow. Tomorrow, your tutelage begins." And thus, he obeyed.

The next day, Alejandro skipped out on minding the shop in favor of Apollonius' lessons. That night, his father discovered two silk neckties had been stolen. He beat the boy so severely for his carelessness that Alejandro's ears rang for two weeks. After that, Apollonius began sculpting mud people, then enchanting them to look like Alejandro. He would set them free an hour before dawn. Then, each morning, when Alejandro went to unlock his father's linen shop, they would switch places.

Liberated, Alejandro would tear off, down the street,

then up the beach, loving his new relatively stable equilibrium. He still could not dance, but he could try. Alone on the beach, with only Neptune and Apollo for witnesses, and the tide for tempo, he could certainly try.

The golems could not speak and returned to dust at sunset, but they tended the store proficiently during the day. And since it was still assumed that Alejandro was mute, no suspicion arose.

The eye Apollonius had forged was the work of a god and, therefore, perfect. By adjusting the lens, Alejandro could filter through all the hues that make up mortals and immortals alike and thereby determine their nature. This served Alejandro well when choosing how best to approach people. Nothing of their character could remain hidden from him, with one exception. No matter how Alejandro screwed up his pupils and adjusted, Apollonius' lifeforce defied definition. He was like starlight, pulsing, growing close, then receding. Thereby, the true nature of the old hermit remained a mystery.

The prism sat directly over Alejandro's real eye. It was enchanted to display a false retina that mimicked the actions of the other one. Finally, he no longer appeared cross-eyed and was much more handsome. With time, Alejandro made an exceptional apprentice. And Apollonius, apart from his bouts of moodiness, forgetfulness, and childlike behavior, made for a wise mentor.

But as the boy grew, so did his ambitions. He wanted to travel to the island city of Pandemonium, which at that time was considered the intercontinental capital of magical arts. Yet, he could not find a way to express this to Apollonius. And in silence, his ambition fermented to poison. He began to resent the old man's emotional outbursts and forgetful nature until, eventually, he began to consider robbing him of his gold and setting sail in the night for Pandemonium.

But first, before betraying Apollonius, he decided to try reasoning with him to alleviate some of his guilt. He asked his teacher, "Do you realize how much wealth you have hidden in this cave? If we took only a small portion of this gold into the village ... " but the old man interrupted him.

"... it would swallow and destroy everything sacred about it." Then Apollonius stood and tromped into an adjoining cavern. The boy sulked off. Dejected, yet undefeated, he ponderously called aloud, "Will the village remain destroyed?"

"No—," came the response, "but it will remain desolate for far longer than you'd care to live!"

"I want to live forever, like the great magicians of Pandemonium are said to."

Apollonius returned to the main cavern red-faced. Alejandro's offhand comment had visibly dug beneath the old man's pride. After a flustered moment of gathering himself and stumbling on false starts, he called back, "The magicians of Pandemonium are true magicians, indeed, if they have you convinced that they will live forever." And it was left at that. But Alejandro continued to dream of the city; he couldn't prevent that. And what sin can exist in a foolish child's dreams? But it was in action that Alejandro sinned; Or—perhaps not. After all, Alejandro only sought to fulfill the promise he had made to his master that he would one day slay him.

Beneath the next tiger moon, at high tide, Alejandro swam the seawater expanse separating his village's beach from the god's gullied marsh. As he trekked, he could hear reptiles slither beside his feet, and the thorny thistles of the undergrowth tore his breeches, making him bleed. He could not see well. He could not see, but it didn't matter; there was only one direction to travel. And as long he didn't cry out, come thorn, or snake's venom, he would reach the cave.

When he reached its mouth, he whispered a spell to diminish his size so he could pass through its narrow entrance chute without struggling and causing a commotion. When he reached the grand hall, he barely remembered to cast a spell of levitation, to not awaken the slumbering god with the clatter of trotting on gold.

Finally, standing at the head of his master's great oaken bedframe, Alejandro raised the cudgel high into the air before bringing it down atop Apollonius' skull with a wet smack. He immediately released the handle and stumbled backward onto his ass; then crab crawled to a corner. In disgust and horror at his actions, he placed his head into his hands and began to sob miserably.

Then, after a time, a quiet gurgling voice coaxed, "It's alright, young one." There came a twisting sound, then a pop as Apollonius snapped his dislocated jaw back into place. He had a hole in the center of his forehead that made him look like a cracked eggshell. Then, Apollonius took a great breath, and when he exhaled, granules of crushed white bone, like salt, began to rebuild themselves. A sandy coastline reverted to a rocky cliff, and Apollonius' bones were whole again.

Slowly, quietly, the god stood and came to Alejandro's side. He plopped down on the cavern floor and joined him in staring into the darkness. His face was the dark shadow of distant space, vastly empty and full of holes. He said, "I cannot be killed by a mortal. Only another god, or possibly a great holy man can take my life. And I am far too ashamed to ask another god to help me commit suicide. When you found my hideout, I knew you were special. I saw a way out. So, I selfishly trained you, hoping one day you would be strong enough to kill me. Like the devil, I tempted you with knowledge, power—even this," he said, holding out a handful of the golden coins for examination, "Evil, which I despise so entirely. This gold is a curse that has bound me to this cave for six centuries. You see, I was young too once ... maybe a few times. In my ambitious youth, I used my powers to collect this gold. Now that I am old and know what a curse wealth can be, I have not the heart to pass it on to even my greatest enemy." Then, his face once more reverted to that of an infant as he began to weep.

Alejandro felt pity for the god. Placing an arm over his shoulder, he said, "I can try again tomorrow?"

Apollonius gave a sad little smile. "It is of no use. As soon as I sense the injury of my bones collapsing, I regain consciousness and instantly begin to heal." Then they both sat quietly in the darkness for many hours. At dawn, sleep overtook Alejandro. He collapsed and did not reawaken until the energy pulse from the following evening's green flash shuddered him back to life. However, Alejandro chose not to fully open his eyelids; instead, he stealthily surveyed the room. Once he was sure Apollonius was not home, Alejandro stood and began fumbling through Apollonius' toiletries, until he found a sewing needle. This he stored in his pocket, then returned to the place he had previously lain and pretended to sleep. Once Apollonius returned from the beach, Alejandro did not move until Apollonius was safely snoring in bed.

With Apollonius snoring, Alejandro crept to his master's bedside. He was happy to find Apollonius' boots were already laid out on the floor and would not require removal. He did, however, struggle for an hour to delicately unfurl Apollonius' thick woolen socks without waking him. It was a job that would have been impossible without the precision sight of his prism.

Next, he took the sewing needle from his pocket and lightly dragged its point along the sole of Apollonius' heel until a thin band of shimmering saltwater began to seep from the wound. After this, Alejandro carefully replaced his master's socks, exited the cave, and swam home over the midnight tide to wait out the darkened hours. Alejandro was dead tired from the swim, but he could not sleep.

The next day, when he returned to the cave to receive his regular lessons, Apollonius was all aflutter, gliding this way and that, from cavern to cavern, obsessively tidying. He would not speak to Alejandro, at least not in cohesive words forming decipherable thoughts. He was sweating and red from exertion—dusting corners, stacking books, and sweeping the floor, seemingly, all at once.

This hardly seemed to make any sense, as there was a belly of saltwater forming at the base of the cave and slowly rising. Alejandro went from cavern to cavern checking, but it was not washing in from the ocean. The water only rose to Alejandro's ankles, but this was dangerously high for Apollonius, who appeared to have seeped liquid from his heel until eventually shrinking to the diminutive height of approximately a foot and a half tall and shrinking rapidly.

Though Apollonius' temperament appeared elated, Alejandro felt wrought with guilt. He dropped to his knees beside Apollonius and cried, "Master, it was me. I have done as you asked and slain you. Now, please absolve me of your murder. Also, forgive me for the future sin of taking your gold, which I know I will do."

At this, Apollonius "Pfffphed" with disbelief, retorting, "Have I taught you nothing? Take my money? Only a fool would want money."

But searching his desires, Alejandro knew that he did want the gold, so he said as much, asking, "Master, what if I am a fool?"

Then, Apollonius lost his composure, and began to laugh, and sputtered saltwater from his mouth so profusely that he nearly went underwater in the process. But Alejandro quickly gathered what was left of his rapidly dissolving mentor between his palms. Even then, he continued to drip and escape between his fingertips.

"Then you are a fool, Alejandro. That is okay. I have been that too. And what a fool must do now is gather this treasure and set sail for Pandemonium. Become a great wizard. Learn many new things—whatever their end." Then he paused to laugh. "It does not matter what else you do. But heed my warning and do not pass through your village with this gold in your possession."

Alejandro felt relieved that his master had accepted his choice. But then a doubt crossed his mind, and he asked, "Apollonius, have I done it? Have I slain you, master?"

"No," Apollonius admitted, eyes downcast. "And yes. I have poured myself into you, and you swallowed me like hungry sand. So, how can I die? In time you will see, there is never a lack of substance, only the delusion of scarcity. Minds like your father's, full of Hel, obsess over matters of death and property. Oh, the things these imbeciles could learn from the purity of being a jackass who must rely on the rain and sun for their next meal. Now there is a lesson to dispel fear. Live unafraid, Alejandro. Goodbye, my beloved fool. And with that, Apollonius disappeared into droplets, and Alejandro was once again alone.

**Dear Jodo,**

When you became the father of the midnight movie in 1970 following the success of your cult classic, the Mexican Acid Western *El Topo*, you were already 39 years old, and previously, primarily a theater director. You entered middle age and international stardom simultaneously. At the time, this may have seemed like an unusually late age to start a new career, but today, you have more than doubled that age and only continued to evolve. Your failure to cease growing and become, as you described in your book *Psychomagic*, a respected, lodged monolith opposing the river's flow, has resulted in new risks, such as your two biopic films: 2013's *La Danza de la Realidad* and 2016's *Poesía Sin Fin*, representing some of your best work to date.

How is this possible?

I've come to only one conclusion: time works differently in the Jodoverse.

But my real reason for mentioning your age is to say that you had an entire career before becoming the father of the midnight movie, as a poet, actor, clown, mime, therapist, master of ceremonies, father, and theater director. And to exclude your time in Paris spent learning the art of mime from Marcel Marceau and founding the Panic Movement would be detrimental to your character development.

At this point in our story, you are not the cowboy rogue you portray in *El Topo*—yet. You are still a young, hot-blooded man in Paris or Pandemonium.

One more thought ...

The first of your work I ever encountered was the 1973 film *The Holy Mountain*. You can imagine my confusion. But midway through the film, in one particular scene, I found my compass rose, which gave me my bearings. It was the scene where the warrior, Axon, ordered his army of castrated men to open fire on a group of peaceful protestors. I had wondered if this scene was inspired by the Tlatelolco Massacre of 1968, when the Mexican army opened fire on 5000 peaceful political reformists.

I found this compass in the mangled dying bodies of these reformists.

At the start of the scene, when the gunfire began and the protestors started to fall, the special effects were moderately realistic. Then, as the scene progressed, I realized that some of the gore looked phony. And I wondered, did the studio run out of money at this point? Next, the victims started coughing up grapes instead of blood, and their guts spilled fruit instead of intestines. It was hilarious. It was entirely absurd. Finally, a dying girl's body opened up to release a white pigeon, and suddenly, death was beautiful again.

The scene was like your voice inserted into the action telling me, stop watching the film, stop listening to the words, and pay attention to what I am trying to show to you! Since that scene, I have never been lost in one of your narratives.

*“I have sold my devil to the soul.”*

-Poesia Sin Fin

# Chapter 2:
# Pandemonium

Alejandro, being both blinded by grief and exceedingly foolish, did not heed Apollonius' advice not to take any of the gold into his village. But it was not for himself that he disobeyed. Alejandro felt enormous guilt about leaving his aging father without a hand to mind the shop. So, he returned to the village with one bag of the eerily luminescent gold slung over his shoulder, hidden in a knapsack.

He only spent one more night beneath his parents' roof, though he did not sleep. He rose early when his mother did, long before sunrise, while his father still slept. Approaching her, Alejandro attempted to gather her bony limbs in a farewell embrace. But she pushed him off, waving him away, calling, "If you have so much energy, why don't you go to the market early to get your mother some tomatoes and chile petines for dinner tonight."

Next, Alejandro crept into his father's room. Standing above him, he perceived his father as a hideously distorted version of himself. The man was a tight ball of scars, a lifetime of accumulated slights and wounds, yet, unto himself, he remained undefeated. But at what cost? His white eyes rolled tirelessly even as he slept, and occasionally he would sit upright and curse at a specter in the corner of his room.

Alejandro slid the bag of gold between his father's work boots and his bed, so it would be the first thing he saw when he woke. Then he lingered, feeling a sense of great pride about having provided his father with his deepest desire. It was a good gift, Alejandro insisted to himself, even as deep foreboding settled into his stomach. But he resolved, "My father is as foolish as me. Who am I to deny him his dreams of wealth and power?" And with that, Alejandro put behind him his past life, his time spent as a mute, all the embarrassing rumors of his madness, and set sail aboard a spice trading ship bound for Pandemonium Isle.

As his home shrank to a dot on the horizon, did the boy look back?

Many times. But still, the man moved forward towards his destiny.

This tale is not complete without at least mentioning the extreme risk of sailing at this point in history. The year was 1946. The second great war had just ended. Nazi Germany had fallen. But it was rumored, if not known, among the local fishers and traders that Adolf Hitler's final order had been to send his entire subaquatic fleet to their secret bunkers in South America, particularly off the coast of Peru and Chile.

German U-boats were the least of the sailors' worries. Missile-laden, tremendous underwater machines' movements created currents rendering the ocean hellishly volatile. Sailors feared the iron behemoths, Hitler's experimental napalm breathing sea dragons that could swallow mid-sized ships whole and convert their steel and blood to fuel. But luckily, there were no Nazi sightings during Alejandro's journey. And he arrived at the sprawling fish-gut-scented port of Pandemonium unharassed.

Stepping ashore, Alejandro was shocked by the sight

of a looming naked satyr, a massive hairy brute leaning against a post on the dock wearing only sunglasses. His testicles were the size of oranges. "Kid! I've been expecting you," he called. "I am the great God Pan. Welcome to my city, the capital of the arts. You will find it is dangerously easy to fall in love in and with my city. I named it after my greatest love."

Alejandro, having never left his small village, did not know if it was customary to be greeted upon arrival by none other than the city's founder. But being both young and foolish, he took the gesture in good faith.

Pan was a festive, overwhelming presence who possessed magical powers of suggestion through gesture—an art Alejandro was keen to learn. With a few motions, Pan demonstrated his abilities by enchanting a hapless porter who was unloading the ship into believing himself entrapped within a prison made entirely of air. The poor fellow was unable to move and thought he was suffocating until Pan drew a door on the cell to release him.

Next, he pulled a similar illusion on Alejandro. The moment Alejandro stepped from the wooden docks to the cobblestone, puke-strewn street, he appeared in a dirty pale pink bar with stools the color of old crushed grapes. The bar was furnished like a seventeenth-century French brothel. A mixture of pornographic and violent imagery lined the walls. And draped across nearly every red lip-shaped sofa writhed some creature, or another in various states of dehydration and nudity, moaning, still recovering from the party the night prior.

Pan handed the boy a mug of something foamy and sweet, and said, "In Pandemonium, never tell yourself no. There is no urge you must deny yourself. Here, there is no need for Logos, only nature, and the bravery to act upon it. When you arrived, I sensed great power arrived with you. Pandemonium is a good place to be powerful. All the more, if you have a powerful ally."

Then he clinked Alejandro's mug in forced agreeance, and they both raised their glasses. As Alejandro drank, Pan held the bottom of Alejandro's glass higher and higher, forcing him to finish his beer in one drag. Another was instantly presented. Their glasses clinked again, and the ceremony repeated.

"Only the first one was free," Pan warned. "When you arrived, I also smelled all the gold you're hiding from me. Don't worry. I'm not going to rob you. You're good for our economy. Pandemonium is a good place to be wealthy. Especially if you have a friend who can teach you how to spend it."

Glasses clinked. More followed. Thus began the two-and-a-half-year orgy of senses during which Pan taught Alejandro the power of gesture, persuasion, trickery, and chaos magic. He learned that there was no manner of lust that he needed to deny himself. His gold ensured every manner of beauty and filth kept flowing into the bar to be consumed, fucked, then left to rot. The piles of past kept amassing, and no one was sweeping, as Alejandro's taste grew ever more perverse under Pan's tutelage.

The party never ceased; the trash continued to pile up. Beer bottles, sacrificed animals, the bones of chickens consumed feathered and whole, the spines of great fish from the depths picked clean as popsicle sticks. When the space beneath the partygoer's feet became crowded, they would merely step higher atop the mound. And so, the rot grew taller daily, eventually becoming a black tower, a monument to excess that was visible from every corner of Pandemonium.

One day, when feeling rather careless, Alejandro decided to play a trick on Pan. While the god slumbered, Alejandro constructed an immaterial closet full of moth-balled sweaters and locked him inside. Then he brought a frying pan and began clanging it against the wooden construct. When Pan awoke, he was confounded. He rammed his horns into the seemingly wooden walls and found them impenetrable. Then he began bellowing curses that turned to purple and black spells, but they ricocheted around the closet singeing Pan's mane, only serving to enrage him further. From outside the closet, the construct was transparent, and Alejandro rolled around the floor in laughter.

The god did not find a way to dispel the illusion, and Alejandro eventually removed the enchantment. But then, seeing Pan's fury, he became quite terrified.

"Now!" the god thundered somewhere between pride and rage, "I suppose this was your way of showing me you have mastered my teachings?" Then a smile peeked through. "I couldn't have weaved a better enchantment myself. With these tools, you will never need to accept 'no' for an answer again."

The sentiment initially troubled Alejandro, but with time, he came to recognize its truth. With the right combination of words and gestures, a person's will could be made to turn, run backward, and trample them. The principles of universal oneness and solipsism look terrifyingly complementary when displayed from a particular skew. Alejandro could bend his subject's mind to that skew. In his heart, he believed he held no accountability and did not know if he ever wanted to again. But even when he was bereft of meaning, he knew he was not empty. Some actions were individually him, like signs of life in a corpse. For instance, he continued to pay his bar tab and the full price for hookers though there was no need. He wondered at that. Was this an immutable aspect of his nature, a sign of his inherent goodness, or merely a remaining artifact of Apollonius, or even Christ lodged in his mind like an undigested breadcrumb?

Brain, or soul?

Alejandro learned to despise conscious thought.

Who was he?

Brain, or soul?

The answer was incomplete in one and ethereal in the other.

Who was he?

He certainly was no longer the boy fearfully staring backward at his village as it disappeared on the horizon like a lost puppy. Now, whatever he was, he must be his own. Currently, Alejandro only wanted to move forward to find the next thing, behind the next thing, beneath the next.

Insatiable—thus was his state of mind at the end of those two and a half years, soon to be bookmarked by Alejandro's twentieth birthday.

Pan wanted to mark the occasion, and Pan did not believe in subtlety, announcing the event from atop the wooden bar, drunkenly swaying, threatening to collapse and possibly gore his audience. He slurred, "Now, does ever-ee-one in Panda-monium loooove our little treasure thief, Ale ... buyer of the drinks?"

A great cheer arose from the crowd, and Alejandro

beamed like a county fair pig. Then Pan asked, "How much do you love Alejandro?"

The crowd fell inexplicably silent. Alejandro's pride was wounded. But Pan remained unperturbed, as he'd expected this response, continuing, "Tomorrah, for my Alejandro's birfday present, I'ma make him like me—a god. Alejandro, I will name you—god of trickery."

Alejandro noted that the crowd's reaction was a mixed bag, some cheering, some whispering. There was no consensus. For most mortals, the prospect of becoming a god was beyond imagining, but again, Alejandro was a fool. From the moment he'd first met Apollonius, he'd dreamt of becoming immortal. And was that such a sin? He wondered. Then, Pan's words returned to him, "In Pandemonium, there is no urge you must deny yourself." And Alejandro decided, if I am a fool, I can only walk forward to become wise.

It was settled.

The ceremony was prepared. Women and children from neighboring villages were captured and transported up the coastline to the black tower, where Pan's barkeep paid top dollar for the slaves, but only on credit. After all, the slavers thought, after the big event, the barkeep would be swimming in gold.

The tower's smell of decay could not be masked. But the liquor was stocked, cocaine dispensers placed at every doorway, and the swimming pool pumped with LSD, which would soak into the participating swimmers' skin because, among hardened partiers, ambiance is not nearly as important as party favors.

Over the past two and a half years, Alejandro's physical appearance had fallen by the wayside. Over time,

Alejandro had even come to resemble a beast. Because of his lingering vertigo, Alejandro had taken to traveling on all fours. In the mornings, before he started drinking, Alejandro would climb down, then up from the side of his tower to visit the town like a great ape. His skin had become plump from constant feasting, and yet his eyes had grown sallow with boredom and malaise. Catching his reflection in the mirror behind the bar the morning of the ceremony, he thought, this is not the way a god should behave. Or perhaps, it is only not the way a god should look. Maybe I should choose to become part animal, possibly coyote, like the native's trickster god.

The party began with light appetizers as not to sour the participants' vigor for the post-ceremony orgy with unexpected flatulence and cramps. Then, it was time for the ceremony. Pan threw an empty wine bottle at the liquor cabinet behind the bar, and two bottles exploded beside a freshly abducted bartender's face. She screamed and dropped to the floor.

Pan spoke with the air of a circus ringleader, addressing the crowd, "Friends! You have just witnessed the first two ceremonial rites of the evening. In one stroke, I poured out the sacrificial liquor and made a virgin orgasm."

Raucous laughter ensued. Humiliated, the bartender chose not to rise.

"Now we have only the third sacrifice to make. Then our friend will become immortal, to rule forever by my side as my lieutenant." The crowd cheered. Pan continued, "In a good mood, are we? Then, I will ask you again. How much do you love Alejandro?" And again, the tower fell silent. Pan alone continued to chuckle. His chuckle grew to a roar. Eventually, he parceled out, "Pieces of shit, all of you! That is why you are my people." There were a few nervous fits of laughter, which Pan silenced. "Relax, my scum. None of you must die today! I tasked my barkeep ahead of time. And what do you know? Your god provides."

At this, an armored team of musclebound dwarves forced a captured chain gang of women and children to enter and line up beside the bar's stage like an auction was about to take place. Then Pan lit a cigar, and in a measured voice, said, "The first lesson of being a god is a god must learn to judge. So, Alejandro, my friend, choose your sacrifice."

But Alejandro could not answer. Something had caught his eye: the lifeforce emanating from one of the children in the lineup. It was strangely familiar, like a powerful beam of light cast from a great distance. Alejandro filtered through his prism's lenses, then realized that like Apollonius' lifeforce, the child was actively masking its essence. But focusing on the child was like a drug, and the child's calmness trapped Alejandro in a deep trance that forbade movement. But Pan did not see this exchange.

Angry at his inaction, Pan bellowed, "In Pandemonium, there is no urge which you must deny yourself!" And this entered Alejandro's mind as well, where he judged it authentic. So, he plunged in deeper to search his soul. In his interior, he found that Pan was right about this, as well as something else: there was an urge within him. It was there, lodged deep in his unconscious, immutable and hard as a diamond. Alejandro judged it would be a sin against his internal divinity not to let it out.

He said, "Pan, my friend, there is so much you have taught me that I love, but not this. This is something I do not want to do. I know that about myself."

Pan's expression boiled into a dangerous amalgamation of fuming and playful. He crossed the floor to Alejandro without taking a step and was now towering above him. But Alejandro was unafraid, knowing this was only an illusion that Pan had taught him himself. And he said, "I have judged that for my birthday, I would like to set these captives free."

The dwarves looked unsure as Alejandro approached the captives, selected the small boy with black hair who'd emanated such a strange lifeforce, and began untying him. But they were too afraid to interfere, as it was known throughout Pandemonium that Alejandro had become quite the magician, and not a threat to take lightly. Also, as Pan often bemoaned, cowardice was rampant among Pandemonians, as all residents feared death to an unnatural degree, yet all fantasized about killing everyone they ever met.

Alejandro was stooped, untying the child, as Pan huffed black smoke. He would not warn the young wizard when he charged, seeking to gore him by surprise and watch his lights fade at the tip of his horns.

Then, Pan began his charge.

The child Alejandro was untying began to bloat. He bloated two, then seven, settling at last at twelve times his original size. The growth spurt caught Alejandro by surprise, and he tumbled backward safely into a heap.

Pan's charge did not falter. His horns pierced the child's now gelatinous form, and he continued to press forward until he was engulfed within the child's body, where he became lodged. The child's massive belly was now semi-translucent from the outside, like Alejandro's closet spell, allowing the crowd a firsthand view of the struggling satyr's misfortune. The guests laughed as Pan ripped with his claws and thrashed his horns, but the child's innards seemed to regrow like vines as fast as Pan could slit them loose.

Recovering to his knees, Alejandro gazed up, and though he'd never seen one, he understood that this was an enlightened being, a creature of single purpose, the Bodhisattva himself.

"Buddha?" Alejandro asked unsurely.

And the massive, soft face gave an affirming smile. Then his mouth began to twist as if about to puke. And out of his stomach, burst a raging, indignant Pan. Wobbly cubes and maimed strands of something that looked like lemon Jell-O hung from Pan's horns as he glared from Alejandro to Buddha, his disgust apparent. Alejandro knew he was done for.

Pan yelled up at Buddha, "Oh, fuck you, man. What are you even doing here?" Then, without waiting for an answer, the satyr gurgled a cry of bloodlust and charged back into Buddha's guts. They immediately healed, trapping the enraged satyr once more. Alejandro watched stupefied as his former friend and mentor continued carrying out this illogical cycle of breaking free, becoming further enraged, then mindlessly charging back in like it was a new idea. Pan could not help himself.

Then Buddha spoke, saying in a voice that did not travel from his lips, "Thus is the cyclic nature of a god. We are as tedious as we are sacred. We are imprisoned like mile markers for humans to traverse between throughout life over and over again." His face again became pained. Pan burst forth, turned, and immediately charged in. It was a pitiful sight. It was apparent that Buddha was no more capable of defeating Pan than Pan was of vanquishing Buddha. But still, Alejandro could sense the Buddha's power. He was many times more powerful than himself, even more potent than Apollonius. Hoping he had found a new mentor, Alejandro begged, "My lord Buddha, you have bested my former mentor, proving your superiority. Therefore, I wish to pledge my loyalty to you entirely." Then Alejandro lowered his head, and pinched his eyelids shut to wait for a reply,

... and he waited.

Eventually growing annoyed, Alejandro gave up and raised himself from the ground where he met the wonderfully calm eyes of the Buddha. The sense of peace emanating from him quieted Alejandro's spirit once more. Still, the Buddha did not speak,

... and Alejandro waited.

When things became awkward, Alejandro dared to try again, asking, "May I have the honor of knowing my new master's proper name?"

The Buddha did not look like he would answer. Then after a time, he began to work his mouth in tiny promising circles. Eventually, he spoke with elongated vowels, resting on each syllable; words like airy breath whispered, "I am no one," which much disappointed Alejandro. Yet still, his devotion persevered. He decided to give his new master another try by asking, "Teacher, how shall I live?" At which, Buddha's eyes became alight. Alejandro's anticipation grew alongside Buddha's grin. In his excitement, the Buddha became nearly present, causing his form to solidify and crush Pan, who cursed in agony. Then the Buddha licked his lips, leaned forward, and enunciated carefully this time, using his own mouth, "Reduce suffering." Then he sat back with a look of self-satisfaction and retired to nodding and looking magnanimous.

All was silent. All was zen besides Alejandro, who felt like the only idiot at a party who didn't get a joke. He fought off embarrassment to awkwardly ask, "Is that it?" But Buddha only smiled and allowed his head to lull back and forth in content affirmation.

Pan chose that instant to burst free again from Buddha's belly. This time, he addressed Alejandro directly, calling, "Don't listen to that asshole, kid. He wants to take everything from you—to reduce you until you are nothing and no one, just like him. Arrrr!" He turned back to Buddha, and charged again, once more being absorbed.

Alejandro stared at Buddha. There was no lie in him. So, he asked him plainly, "Is Pan telling the truth? Do you mean to make me no one?"

Buddha continued to smile and nod like a ship cresting calm waves. His enthusiasm didn't increase or decrease—it just was.

"And—are these my only two paths?" Alejandro asked.

Buddha shrugged. This time, his voice was telepathically beamed into Alejandro's mind. "There might as well be only two paths. I have never seen power come from the center, only the extremes. The center is full of hungry ghosts grappling for it and squelching it in the process."

Then, for a time, Alejandro sat cross-legged before the Buddha, meditating. He did not move. He decided he would not move until sure he had heard his own spirit speak. Then, when it did, he replied:

"I want to reduce suffering. This is my purpose, as well. I want to be the perfected archetype, and yet—not quite. I no longer believe purpose is all there is to being. I realized this when I reached for the bottom of myself. I lifted my bucket, and I chose to pour until no more would drain. I wanted to send everything I am back out into the universe and become no one, like you. But there was a problem. When I turned over what should have been an empty bucket, I still saw my reflection. I was immutable. And I realized, I cannot be nobody because I still see Alejandro Jodorowsky at the bottom of that bucket. To claim to be nobody, or anyone else, would be a lie. And that lie would only produce more pain, a growing well of suffering, if only within my own soul. And for this reason, I do not know how I will serve you. Great Buddha, please enlighten me. What am I to do?"

Then the great Buddha straightened his back, drawing himself to his full height. He centered his pupils, appearing most royally zen. And in a booming voice, he proclaimed, "Reduce suffering." Then sat back with that same self-satisfied smirk and bobble-headed nod.

Annoyed, Alejandro rose to his feet, slapped the dust from his knees, and walked out of Pan's bar, calling behind him, "Well, you are no use. Reduce suffering, indeed!"

**Dear Jodo:**

In a distant time, I purchased a comic compilation of reprints titled *Taboo 4*. Back then, it was the only place I could find a copy of your 1978 comic, *Les Yeux*. I wanted to see the first result of your infamous collaborations with the legendary comic artist Jean "Moebius" Giraud. I suppose I was also morbidly curious to read your initial raw reaction to the failure of *Dune*, before the 1980 birth of *The Incal*.

The comic was nearly wordless, more of an idea than a plot. The thought was of being a blind girl seeking new eyes, namely, the eyes of a cat. The sentiment was clear: you purposefully needed to seek out a new way of seeing things. The tale was tender and sad, but it was the disclaimer the publisher added at the end of your story that hurt most.

"Unfortunately, Jodorowsky's *El Topo* is unavailable for either video or theatrical screening, and has been inaccessible to an entire generation."

Was this true? I looked at my entertainment system, suddenly supremely grateful for my collection of your work. It shocked me because *El Topo* was a great success and is still probably your best-known film. John Lennon even loved it.

How did you simply let this injustice go? Why did you not put down your pen, collapse your director's chair, and trade it for a suit to wear to court and fight for the film's distribution rights? It could have been a lovely hill to die upon. But instead of fighting for what could have been, you would not cease to create.

I read a quote you gave shortly after the release of your

first film, *Fando Y Lis,* in which you said, "I have directed many plays simply for clothing and food ... It is better to put your efforts into a film so that even if it is censored, it can be stored away in cans. It may sit for 20 years, but one day it will be seen." Subsequently, that film was lost for 30 years. But I doubt you minded that either. You see, I see you as a poet first, a healer second, a theatrical director third, and then, a film director. I know you have many other talents and titles, but let us not be greedy. Suffice to say, you are a true artist. And any artist in communion with the gods knows that neither their thoughts nor words belong to them. We are like the dream's couriers; our minds become their chrysalis where they dwell until they are birthed. Then, they are ours no longer. And this is just as well. As you said in *La Danza de la Realidad*, "At the end of time, when all matter returns to its origins, you and I will have just been memories, nothing real. Something is dreaming us. Embrace the illusion. Live!"

*“Too much perfection is a mistake.”*

-El Topo

# Chapter 2 ¾:
## Integration

Alejandro sulked through the streets aimlessly, feeling disenchanted, and more lost than ever. What purpose were wizardry and powers now that he'd seen all possible endings, and none were any good? Perhaps, he thought, this is why the gods created mortals powerless. Maybe it was a kindness to obscure the hopelessness of existence.

In the street, Alejandro passed a bearded preacher with rancid breath calling aloud, "Hear me, people! Repent. For you are full of sin and deserving of great judgment and damnation! For shame!"

"Get down from there, you old fool," Alejandro called. This caught the preacher's attention, and he abandoned his post to follow Alejandro. For several blocks, he trailed him, shouting, "Oh, powerful wizard. I'm sure you have done much harm in your life. But have no fear. I am selling wrist and ankle irons made of 100% pure silver. Even a god could not break these chains. Now, all you must do is chain yourself to a mountainside somewhere private where you can't hurt anybody and wait for the end of the universe."

"Get away from me," Alejandro shouted, "Or I will turn you into something nasty, you ... you Villain!"

The insult seemed to meet its mark, leaving the dusty preacher genuinely appalled. He sputtered smelly breath and spat for a while before eventually sounding out, "And what is my crime?"

"The stealing of lives," Alejandro decreed.

The preacher gripped his heart, apparently stunned by

the accusation. "I am not stealing lives, but saving them and preventing crime."

Now Alejandro turned and held the preacher by his shoulders. Staring into the man's filmy brown cataracts, he screamed, "You are chaining people's souls from within. Because of your tyranny, in this life, they will learn nothing of themselves. You offer eternal life? You only offer eternal lives of unproductive repetition!"

At these words, the preacher's tear ducts began to swell, but he did not look away from Alejandro, which Alejandro appreciated. Then, his countenance entirely melted. He sat on the ground rubbing the balding spot at the center of his head, mumbling, "Oh, that's right. I knew that, once. I must have just forgotten." He began to weep softly, then he began to weep bitterly. His face melted off like wax and reformed as the same countenance, only much younger.

"Apollonius?" Alejandro asked.

The preacher gave a slight, sad nod, and began to wail all the harder—to leak, to melt, to drip until he was hemorrhaging seawater. Alejandro feared that he was about to lose his mentor again as soon as he'd found him. But this was not the case, for the eternally resurrecting god was merely shifting forms. Seawater fed the hungry dirt as his body shrank and changed hues until eventually molding into an adolescent girl with green skin and curly red hair. Even her robe had changed from an ashen grey to a rich mahogany brown that hung loosely from her dainty shoulders.

"Apollonius?" Alejandro asked again.

"No. I am Zaratustra now."

"You are a woman," Alejandro stated plainly.

"And you are still a fool," came the response.

Then they both cast illusions to obscure themselves, so they could walk through the marketplace unharassed and speak freely without fear of being overheard by petty magicians. As they walked, Alejandro bore his soul.

"I am still a fool, teacher. And I am more lost than I've ever been. I have lived two lives now. First, I lived for others by serving my family; then, I lived completely for my own pleasures in Pandemonium, but both rang untrue. At least when I was ignorant, life still held some intrigue. There were things left to try. Alcohol and drugs were sacred pleasures, and sex was a gift, a treasure to be won. Now, the world is at once so much less and more. I think I would rather be dumb."

Alejandro sank into self-pity. Then two pale thin-boned hands, now sizably larger than before, lifted his head to meet her hazel brown eyes. Zaratustra was now a beautiful young woman, nearly Alejandro's age. "Then it is a good thing you are still a fool," she said, and slapped him hard across his cheek.

"What do you mean?" Alejandro demanded, rubbing his cherrying cheek.

"I mean, your journey has just begun; you will see. And don't worry; you will not evolve into Buddha. You have already proven that to yourself. Neither will you become Pan because you have discovered your intrinsic moral boundaries. In so doing, you have begun to map your trans-dimensional true form. When the map is complete, you will be whole."

As they passed a fruit vendor, Zaratustra grabbed two pears, tossed one to Alejandro, and continued to walk. "Through your experiences with Buddha and Pan, you have discovered one of the mighty axes on which reality turns." She raised her right index finger to fortify her point. "Only one. You don't know any of the others, and you have no idea how many spokes exist."

"Will you teach them to me, master?"

"After you just so passionately pled to remain dumb? I would never be so cruel! They are yours to discover."

For a time, they trekked side by side in silence. When Alejandro turned again to Zaratustra to speak, she had significantly aged, now wearing a wiry tuft of grey hair atop her stooped frame. He asked her, "Teacher, why are you so wise sometimes and foolish others? Why does your face keep shifting?"

She did not respond for a long time. So long, that Alejandro grew embarrassed for asking. Then when she spoke, her voice crackled like distant static. "My oh-so-very-young pupil, to answer your question would be to illuminate the Euclidian mysteries, which have been lost to humanity for three thousand years." She paused as if finished. Then, an unlabeled bottle of red wine manifested in her hand and popped its own cork, as she said, "I've been dying to tell this tale for ages.

Then they were on the docks. The sun was setting. She passed Alejandro a glass of wine. It tasted smooth and old, like dark berries stored in oaken barrels beneath the deck of some ancient seafaring ship long since petrified.

"These forms I take, each exist inside me as there are many lives inside of you. Humans are the ancients disguised as children. Your short lives and memories are useful for the conversion of energy. You burn bright when you are conflicted. Your struggles to bring balance between your anima and animus, ego and shadow, conscious thought and unconscious intuition, they are all part of a magnificent cosmic engine by which the dead parts of the universe are fed. A field of energy is built up around the globe throughout the day, then pulsed out to feed the stars every night at sunset. This is why the stars only glow at night. You know it as the green flash. It is the entirety of the human purpose, to transform energy through suffering, and in so doing, provide life to the dead."

Alejandro was shocked. But being a fool, in his mind, he still held himself aloft from the fate of the rest of humanity. So, he asked, "Will we ever die, master?"

"No. No one shall. That which is alive shall never die as assuredly as that which is dead shall never live."

"Then where is there hope? Is there any way to escape from suffering?"

"You may choose to become no one like Buddha. You may seek to achieve oblivion through vice. You may become a martyr like Christ. You may also forget your fate at the end of this cycle. Many choose this route accidentally. But I say unto you, until you find and remember your true face, you will never escape the cycle."

Then Alejandro began to beg. "Master, if you love me, how could you leave me to such a fate? Please, tell me how to search for my true face?"

"You do not, fool! Transcendence comes through something similar to muscle memory. The spirit remembers what it earnestly learns. You do not seek transcendence, nor will you find it. This is a waste of time. Instead, live; walk as a fool, and you will learn."

To Alejandro, this seemed acceptable advice. With both dumb pride and awe in his voice, he declared, "I am the only human alive who knows the secret of the Euclidian mysteries."

"Not yet, you don't," Zaratustra replied. Then she put her lips to the bottle and did not retract them until it was empty. "There is still one more part." She stared at the darkening sea and took a deep breath to gather herself before haphazardly blurting out, "The gods are playing humans for fools. There; I said it"

Stunned, Alejandro asked, "Which one of them?"

"All of them."

"How is that possible? Surely one is on our side. Aren't you?"

"I am something else entirely. Perhaps, I will explain it someday. For now, my secrecy must suffice." With a dismissive wave, she moved on. "Alejandro, do you remember the great spokes of reality I spoke of?

He nodded.

"The gods would have you believe that humans wander through their lives, completely in control, attempting to remain faithful to one spiritual ideal or another, but always falling short. And in turn, humans hate themselves for their failings. When in reality, a person's movements are often not the result of their own volition, but a reflection of the movements of the gods themselves. Humans are—humans are like light bulbs, and the gods are like electricity. When a god is nearby, the hapless neighboring humans light up and begin to act in whatever way that particular god exacerbates. Humans do not think in words, they think in symbols, and gods are the manifestation of those symbols. They writhe like snakes in darkness, feeling for empty spaces, expanding where they find no resistance. Their presence can be seen in this dimension in the form of revivals of faith, nationalism, expansionism, and militancy. One god throws a punch in the other's eye, and his fingers become long blades and nuclear missiles. When they spar in close quarters, neighbors kill neighbors. And there is nothing anyone can do to stop them."

As she spoke, Zaratustra's voice had continued to rise. Now, there was something elemental to her, her voice modulating in an inhuman intonation that would have frightened onlookers had she not been enchanted. Then, she came out of the trance and became self-conscious and melancholy, saying, "Now that I have told you this, I don't know how you will choose to go on living." Her pupils quivered back and forth as if searching for somewhere to run. "In fact, I may soon ask you to end my life again as well. You were right. Better to forget. Perhaps this is why we stopped explaining the Euclidian mysteries. I forgot they are such downers."

But Alejandro did not despair, instead choosing to focus carefully upon each of the things Zaratustra had said. Eventually, he replied, "If the gods are moving, then they cannot represent the edges of reality. Do not despair, teacher; you have told me two useful things. First, you taught me that the gods are not limitless; the second leads from the first, that they can, therefore, be surpassed. If they have defined limits of space to move within, then there must be more space, there must be something beyond them. I will find it, master, and that pursuit gives me hope. But first, I must sever the god's control over me. Zaratustra, there must be a way to completely break the gods' hold over me and free myself from the cycle."

Zaratustra appeared middle aged now. The sun was

gone entirely, but still, its afterglow remained. Alejandro noticed the tips of Zaratustra's fingers begin to shimmer; then, another bottle appeared inside her open palm.

She spoke softly. Purposefully. "Alejandro, I can tell you how to free yourself. It will require almost no action from you, yet, it will be the hardest thing you have ever done. Alejandro, a cycle is a circuit composed of more than one individual. Your current incarnation is but a fragment of yourself. If a family cannot come together, then they spiral in opposing directions; the child becomes the antithesis of the parent; nothing changes."

"But, you do not know my father. He will not change. So, am I eternally damned for his failures?"

"No, healing is possible without physical reconciliation. But, if you are to heal yourself entirely, you must also turn and heal your tail."

**Dear Jodo,**

There may be no more important lesson one can learn from you than how to deal with failure. You are not ashamed. In fact, in 2013, you allowed a documentary crew to make an entire film about your most famous failure, entitled *Jodorowsky's Dune*. I still meet people who have never seen a single one of your movies but love this documentary.

It is an unchallenging narrative to follow. The documentary first captivates its audience with a familiar trope, a mad wizard (you) setting off on an adventure. To start, he selects a cast of co-heroes, including Salvador Dali, Orson Welles, Pink Floyd, H.R. Giger, and Moebius—just to name a few. Then, the team sets out on their noble quest to bring Frank Herbert's science fiction novel *Dune* to life. But then, something that never happens in fairy tales occurs. The financial backing falls through, and the film gains a new title: *The Greatest Masterpiece Never Made*.

After seeing the documentary, a person cannot exist without being acutely aware of the *Dune*-shaped hole in their lives. But did your version of *Dune* indeed die? As you say in the film:

> "From this supposed failure came a lot of creation. In life, when things come, you say yes; things go away, you say yes. We don't do *Dune*? Yes! That is: Yes! We don't do it. And then, so what? And then, so what? *Dune* is in the world like a dream. But dreams change the world also."

The story is about more than great ambition and

glorious failure; it is the story of the phoenix. But *Dune*'s rebirth went partially unacknowledged because your project switched mediums, becoming a graphic novel instead of a film.

When I first read your 1980 graphic novel, *The Incal*, I could sense the massive backlog of ideas poured into each of the panels of the book. There are more spiderwebbing ideas in *The Incal* than pages. In my opinion, this universe is larger and more radically populated than *Star Wars*. It is like an over-bloomed fruit tree heavy with its load, dropping ripe fruits that roll into the street and over the neighbor's fence. And many artists have picked from this tree over the years. I will not besmirch the villain's names, but instead, let me cite Brian Michael Bendis' foreword to *The Black Incal*:

> "Listen to me right now! If you are a storyteller from any visual medium on the planet and you are even thinking about nicking something out of this Incal graphic novel collection stop!! Stop it! Stop the madness! Even if you think you are creating an homage ... stop it!"

I suppose I ignored that last line, eh?

The fruits of *Dune* did not end with *The Incal*. They spiderwebbed into follow-ups and spin-offs, including *The Technopriests*, *Megalex*, and my favorite, *The Metabaron* series. The universe, lovingly titled the Jodoverse, is rich with tributaries, each harmoniously flowing back to their headwaters: that ocean inside of your skull. It is that ocean I hear when I read about so-called failed or rather, unfunded Jodorowsky masterpieces like *King Shot* and *Abel*

*Cain*. These are like smiling shells, lain glimmering when the tide pulls back its lips. I know that when the tide returns, the pattern of these teeth may be destroyed, transmuted within the rip curl, but the ideas will remain, and like *The Incal*, they will wait to be reborn.

In my time around other Jodorowsky enthusiasts, I have met tarot readers, psychomagic practitioners, all manner of heretics, and film buffs. Still, there is also another type altogether: the comic fan; and none of them would exist if the film *Dune* had succeeded. But then again, who is to say what would have existed instead? All we can do is say yes.

*"The mole is an animal that digs passages searching for the sun. Sometimes he reaches the surface. When he looks at the sun, he goes blind."*

*– El Topo*

# The King of Chile

When Alejandro's father awoke, his son was already a dot on the horizon, having set sail hours ago for the isle of Pandemonium. But the father was not concerned. At the foot of his bed sat a hefty bag of gold. At that moment, a metamorphosis took place. The man became a new creature, a hungry beast, or perhaps only a more pronounced version of his own shadow. Having now the means to pursue his highest aspiration, he named it for the first time aloud. "I will become the King of Chile!"

The first thing he did was stock his store to the brim. Typically, his backroom was empty. The boxes behind the cash register presented the façade of outpouring linens, while in actuality, they were practically empty, save for the single strands of cloth carefully arranged to hang outside the boxes and give the illusion of fullness. Now each of the baskets, along with new ones, were bulging, as were the customers. Huge, fat people flew in private planes from as far as Mexico to shop in his store. Soon he realized, selling linen to a fat person was four times as lucrative as selling to a local villager. Because of their size, they would need to purchase twice the linen; and because of their wealth, they would only buy an item if it were marked up at least twice its value.

The first new sign Alejandro's father posted in front of his shop read: *No Thin People Allowed*. This sign was quickly joined by a companion below reading: *—Or Poor People*. As he hammered the nails into his signs, he believed he'd realized something profound: Not everyone was necessary, neigh, most people were not. If a store, neigh, a country only catered to its most affluent members, it could become more profitable while outputting less. And this became the platform on which he ran for office, saying, "Progress is forward. If you cannot move forward, then at least do not hinder the winners." And on this slogan, and a pile of money, bribery, and corruption, in the first monarchic revolution of the modern age, Alejandro's father did indeed become King of Chile.

Under the king's reign, Chile was a nation upended and reborn, still struggling to grasp its new identity. It was into these chaotic waters our heretical hero sailed and put into port at his hometown's docks. When Alejandro stepped off the boat, so altered was his appearance by his elongated exposure to magic, that the villagers did not recognize him. To some, he appeared unnervingly similar to their mental manifestation of Christ, while others saw him as a woman nearly identical to the Virgin Mary. But it was unanimously agreed that Alejandro was neither, but a mean-hearted mockery of their faith. So—they sought to burn him.

Being a powerful wizard, Alejandro possessed the power to send the entire mob scattering, transmuted into clucking chickens. But he stayed his hand when he recognized several of his former schoolmates among his attackers. They looked nothing like the simple children he remembered. To his horror, they were mutated, branded by vicious scars, and angry gold clung to their decaying teeth and hung from their necks in chains. Their clothes were manufactured, rather than sewn, yet their feet were still bare.

They were hideous abominations of the villagers

Alejandro remembered, driven mad by possessions and the inevitable paranoia of losing them that follows. They were empty and did not know how to fill themselves. They were fearful, yet wild with hunger, a hunger that no meat could slake.

Recognizing that this plight was of his own making, that he had damned his village years ago by leaving that bag of gold beside his father's bed, Alejandro fell into a deep depression from which he could not be wakened. The wizard lay catatonic with grief. The villagers fell upon him, lashed his hand, and tied him to a stake in the town square. The village butcher was summoned alongside the executioner, for though the people didn't typically consume human flesh, they did obsessively fear harsh winters, famine, and generally anything unforeseeable. For this reason, they had taken to burning each other, and any outsider they could find for the absolute minimal offense. Then, the butcher would cleave the meat from the freshly cooked corpse, salt it, hang it in a smokehouse for a month, and distribute it among the villagers for storage.

Wood and a crowd were being gathering when a trumpet interrupted their exchange, and the mass fell into a panic, knowing the tune announced the arrival of his majesty, the King of Chile. The king's guard charged the town square from the east, on the main road, forcing the crowd to bottleneck against themselves, their homes, and narrow streets, and trample each other in bids to escape. His majesty's guard was composed of 200 castrated homunculi wielding long cattle prods, which they jabbed hard into any ribcage they could find. Once the crowd had been dispersed besides the few brave children hiding out and peeking from nearby windowpanes, all that remained was the butcher. He had been detained because the king wanted to deal with someone personally, and the butcher seemed as reasonably guilty as anyone else.

The king charged at a gallop to within 30 meters of the butcher, then ripped back hard on his horse's reigns. He dismounted to the loud applause of 200 homunculi. Next, he removed his blouse, put up his fist, and dropped into a boxing stance. The executioner, being a giant but mentally inept man, looked confused. He tried politely to leave, but through gesture, it was relayed to him that he must raise his fist as well. Then the battle commenced.

The king made easy sport of the simpleminded man. The giant didn't even have time to fight back. With a couple of well-timed jabs, an uppercut, then a big right-handed haymaker that the butcher didn't even attempt to block, the man was a bruised meaty slab at the king's feet. Then, the king began wildly hopping around like a livid frog calling, "Is there anyone here who would challenge me? Come on! Hear me. I am not only your king; I am the strongest man in Chile—and this is my son." He walked over to Alejandro's catatonic body, lifted, and swung his limp right wrist in the air to identify him; then said, "If anyone has a problem with him, I'll kick their ass. Alright?"

The wizard was collected by the king's guard and ushered in a sunshine-painted carriage to the palace, where he was placed on a bed covered with the most elegant linens money could buy. Alejandro's father believed the boy was merely still frightened from his encounter with the villagers. As far as the king was concerned, this was just another reason to decrease national spending on infrastructure. Why pay for people who didn't even pay him, he thought. Then he comforted himself by picturing his son waking surrounded by such splendor and realizing what a success his father had become. This, his kingdom, would be his great gift to Alejandro. When the boy realizes the security of my power, he thought, he will surely recover quickly.

The king commissioned a harpist to sit by Alejandro's bedside every day and sing songs of his father's greatness, and then, another would enter to do the same but gentler at night. All manner of extravagance was brought to his chamber. There were meals of tiger meat, served with wine made from grapes that were grown with blood instead of water. But it was no use. Alejandro remained as if dead.

His father bellowed; his father mourned; his father spoke great platitudes to the wind, swearing away his kingdom and everything he owned in exchange for his son. Yet, the boy lay still.

Until the night he didn't.

When Alejandro arose, it was the dead of night. He did not alert anyone, but he was hungry. So, he wandered the labyrinthine halls of the palace, hoping to find a kitchen. When he found it, he poured himself a glass of milk, set two pieces of bread on the stove to toast, and sat in the darkness to wait.

At the exact moment Alejandro had awoken, so had the King of Chile, awakened by a terrible dream. In it, he watched crops wither and die, the udders of milking cows squirt pustulous piss-colored bile, and headless chickens that would not perish, but wandered the streets breeding pestilence inside their rotting corpses until at last, they would fall, bloat, and burst, exploding maggots throughout the city.

The king was deeply disturbed by these visions and knew he would not sleep again until he had reminded himself of his own security and wealth. So, as he often did to calm himself, he visited his vault and counted his gold and boxes of other valuables. Afterward, still feeling unsettled, he decided he would dispel his visions entirely with a glass of milk and possibly some toast.

"Drink deeply," Alejandro said to his father from the darkness, startling him. "It may be the last milk you ever have."

"My son!" his father cried and approached with outstretched arms, but Alejandro withdrew, saying, "You may not wish to embrace me once you have heard what I have done."

His father settled nervously into his chair at the head of the table. Alejandro handed him a piece of his toast as he prepared to explain. "To begin, I am the one to blame for this present ... abomination that I once called home. I was a fool to go against Apollonius' wishes and leave you that bag of gold. And for this injustice, my soul required penance. When I first saw what has become of my kin, I became weakened, and the great spider goddess Melancholia snagged me in her web, where she bound my body with eternal silk. Once she was sure I could not escape, she began to sing to increase my suffering, reminding me that there was no amount of personal suffering I could ever endure to atone for my sins upon others. And for a time, this was meant to be my fate, until I thought on her words more carefully. Then I asked her, "if my suffering will never amount to repayment, then is there something else I can do besides suffer to pay my debt?"

This surprised the old spider, who thought she'd heard every plea a mortal could make. I could see the greed glowing in her eyes. She said that while my suffering tasted exquisitely curious, I am just one person. She said that if my pain were spread over a larger area, perhaps all of Chile, then, with a great fire, and a lot of suffering, she could cleanse the world of my mess. When I agreed, she released me.

Alejandro's father cheered with glee. "A great story! Then the old spider is fooled, eh? My son, the trickster. Indeed, you have proven yourself worthy of the honorable name, Jodorowsky!" he exclaimed.

But Alejandro's expression remained distant and unrelieved. Soon the father's joy was tamped by dread. "I fear you misunderstand me, father. There is no trick. I gave her permission to unleash the goddess Hel upon Chile until the land is cleansed. I even had to lend Hel my powers so she could have the energy to manifest her massive scaly form within our dimension. She is coming, father. No one can stop this."

As Alejandro spoke, the King of Chile's chin became heavier and heavier until, at last, he was holding his head in his hands, repeating, "What will I do? How will we survive?"

But Alejandro calmed his father, saying, "Do not be afraid. As you said, you are a very wealthy and powerful man. Surely a king has nothing to fear."

With this, the king's countenance brightened. He became at least the shadow of the man he so avidly tried to embody. His smile beamed forth, his teeth each individually plated with alternating silver and gold. Everything exposed was the opposite of their interior. Yet, he cried aloud with as much pomp as he could muster, "My son! My heir has returned. Let the kingdom burn! We will survive. We are Jodorowskys, are we not?"

And survive they did—for a time. From his walls, the king watched his hellish visions each come true. Reports arrived daily, begging him for help, rations, military aid. Word arrived of 10,000 dead in the East of some mysterious pestilence, while 10,000 died in the West of famine. But the king pulled all his resources inward. Stocking his castle with guards and food, he remained safe in his walls.

Pleading for charity, and with their delegates' letters going unanswered, the peasants began to amass at the palace gates. In response, the king had his homunculi dig a moat around the perimeter and import alligators to patrol it. Still, the peasants amassed at the drawbridge daily, begging for scraps from the king's table. But the king said, "I cannot feed all of them, so I will feed none of them. Better they all go elsewhere and fend for themselves."

A few hundred meters past the castle, there stood a hill, where the peasants could gather and gawk inside the castle's walls. There, they watched fat cows devour hay alongside thoroughbred ponies. Daily, they would watch the horses trollop with their trainers for exercise, then lay languidly, basking in the sun, growing fatter each day. "How are the horses looking? Any fatter?" became a standard sardonic greeting in town. Then the conversation would inevitably turn to discussing their hunger, which would inevitably lead to addressing the injustice of the monarchy. And thus, the sieging army of beggars became protesters, then rioters, and finally, arsonists.

Knowing their king's love of fine linen, the villagers knew his palace must be highly flammable. They gathered their trash from throughout the village and soaked it in gasoline. Then they would stand atop the hill and bend back the adolescent monkey puzzle trees with ropes, load them with trash, set it ablaze, cut the line, and watch their fiery refuse reign down upon their oppressor. All the king's henchmen ran to and fro with buckets of water, putting out fires before they could gain traction. Then one lucky flaming pile of rotten fish and feces landed in the courtyard and set a long-running carpet ablaze. The fire sprinted in a circle along the courtyard, then charged into the palace following the carpet's path. The king was the first to notice the flames when it came to a crossroads in his dining hall and took off from there in three different directions. "After it, you fools," he cried at his dinner guests who were dining at the time.

To their credit, the guests huffed and puffed to chase the flame, unsure what they would do if they caught it, but alas, they were all quite fat and could not hold the chase. Many tapestries, countless hours weavers had spent hunched over their loom, were eviscerated in that hungry instant. Then the king watched his self-portrait catch ablaze, and duelling terror and fury spread through every crack in his old bones. He screamed at his tired gentry, "Get up! Get up, you lazy bums and save my palace, or I will kick all of your asses!" There came no response, only moans. So, he added, "Then I will seize your lands and see you thrown out into the streets to beg. How would you like that?"

While each of the lords did not like this prospect at all,

they were already quite tired from the chase. And being after lunch, they were also somewhat drunk, and the pursuit had given them stomach cramps. The possibility of doing more work seemed overwhelming. So, they collectively decided they would rather die. Believing their king would not turn them out, in solidarity, they all fell asleep with serious plans to deal with the fire problem in the morning.

They were wrong. And the king did not give them until morning. When he found them sleeping, he instantly ordered his guards to escort them outside the walls and leave them there to fend for themselves. Then the king crept to his rooftop to watch what unfolded.

The instant the lords were within the peasants' reach, they fell upon them and lashed them to stakes, which they lined in front of the palace walls. Then, the screaming began, as they were set ablaze. But the peasants were too hungry to wait. So, the butcher began to cut slices off the burning men while they were still screaming. As he cut, he passed the meat along to the crowd.

It was a communal event, a barbeque, and everyone outside the palace walls was in high spirits. One farmer brought into town several barrels of grapes from his fields that had been infested by worms and left to rot and ferment for several months. But because of the famine, because of the hopelessness, because they were jackasses relying on the sun to provide tomorrow's meal, the people didn't care if they would shit themselves rotten in the morning, they were going to get drunk tonight. They ate the meat and drank the barrels dry, not knowing that the worms inside were a powerful hallucinogen.

They began to sing. They brought out all manner of

instruments and percussive tools to perform with. They danced the cueca without ritual, deciding they liked it better that way; then, the bolero too. Things became wild and hedonistic. A woman, wanting to join the dance, tossed her baby into the king's alligator moat. Then, when the alligators came to devour the child, the townspeople swarmed the beast with hatchets, and hoes, and pointed broken broomsticks. Soon all twelve of the alligators meant to protect the king were crudely slain.

The peasants hung the alligators' bodies by their tails from trees and built small controlled fires beneath to simmer them. Then, realizing the moat was no longer to be feared, the villagers dived in and began to bathe, and swim, and fuck, and by some cruel trick of the moonlight, as their skin became pale and clean, to the king's eyes the monsters started to resemble something like the humans he had once lived beside. And the King of Chile was terrified.

He ran to his guards' mount, yelling, "wake up, wake up you lazy bastards! Wake up, or there will not be a tomorrow to wake to. The peasants have taken the moat and are at our gates. We must build higher walls! Begin to build higher! As high as they will stand. We must protect ourselves from Hel."

Wild-eyed, he roused his son, shrieking, "You are a wizard. Cast a spell of protection over my palace. Summon a beast to massacre my enemies!"

To his credit, the wizard did not yawn anywhere but his eyes. "I could ..." he began, then stopped to examine the apple on his bedside. "But, no. That would break the pact I made with the goddess Melancholia. Then you would have both her and Hel to deal with. And as things stand, Hel has already delivered your people. First came Hel, then Pandemonium ensued, and from it, his twin, Buddha, shall be born in the morning. They are each other's shadow. This is enough to restore order, enough for any human to live by—for now. Once the people have passed out from the pleasure of this night, they will dream the delta dream and awaken with their equilibrium restored."

The king raised his eyebrows. "Then she is done with me? She will leave and cease to torment me?"

"Just the opposite, I'm afraid, father. Now that she has purified the land, you are her sole focus."

At this, the king sat on the floor and cradled his knees into his arms. Still, the wizard continued. "They have recognized their shared humanity through mutual suffering, and a common enemy—the plutocracy, namely its head, you, father. As you've said many times, you are the richest, most powerful man in the land; and the strongest. This is good. For at dawn, they will come for you."

"My god!" the king gasped, then scurried out into his halls, screaming, "Bury the food! Bury all the food! We will hide it, so if we must retreat, we can sneak back later and take it. Also—bury the linens. They are very expensive and will help me raise an army to retake Chile when this is all over."

Alejandro sighed in disappointment.

When dawn came, the King of Chile was cowering behind a locked door, sitting atop his safe, surrounded by his favorite linens like a candle waiting to be lit. The king had summoned Alejandro to come help quell his fear of dying without an heir, but the rebellious youth was nowhere to be found. Hours passed, yet neither Alejandro nor the expected invading force arrived.

So, he waited.

And continued to wait.

When Alejandro finally did arrive, he was accompanied by some wretched stooped elderly peasant who claimed he had been elected the people's intermediator.

"As I told you last night, father, the villagers have awoken and recognized each other again. Now the healing can start. They would sue for peace if you would have it?"

Internally, the king began to plot: It will be hard to reacquire my dignity when my son has betrayed my sovereignty so completely, inviting enemies inside my home when I am at my weakest. Luckily, this negotiator is old and feeble. With my strength and the power in my lungs, I will cripple this man with intimidation in no time. He will return to his people having agreed to every term I dictate. Then they will remember why I am the king.

A mean scowl tightened his cheekbones. Then, the king took the deepest breath he could muster. When he opened his mouth, he bellowed, "Heeeee-haw! Hee-haw!"

Then he cleared his throat to try again, but only the neigh of an ass would emerge. It was hopeless. He stared in disbelief from the elderly man to Alejandro, then back again, helpless to communicate.

Turning to the negotiator, Alejandro said, "I am the king's eldest and only son. Tell the people my father is mentally unwell. But he wants no more bloodshed. He will return the palace and its wealth to the people. And in exchange, he asks that he be allowed to graze upon the courtyard grass and sleep in the palace stables."

The king hee-hawed his disapproval, but his demands were not taken seriously. Instead, the dignitary watched, mouth agape, as his king completed his transition into a jackass by lifting his tail and shitting on his pile of gold.

Alejandro's terms were agreed to without amendment. Village life improved, but it did not return to what it was before. There still were bits of luminous green-gold in circulation, but these were balanced by the little Buddha figurines that reminded the people of their better nature.

Soon the royal palace was converted into the new parliament building, and the grounds within the gates became a park with a petting zoo, where for a small fee, the children could feed grain to and ride the King of Chile.

**Dear Jodo,**

Is it true that for any story to end adequately, the hero must first reconquer his beginning?

In his book *Maps of Meaning*, Jungian Clinical Psychologist Dr. Jordan Peterson wrote, "It is the responsibility of every man to rescue his dead father from the underworld." I don't believe many can understand the breadth of such an undertaking as you can. I suspect that after the release of *Tusk* in 1980, it was this very internal familial struggle that broke your nine years of filmmaking silence.

Though *La Danza de la Realidad* was your first film to overtly deal with your childhood trauma, I believe its seeds existed in your 1989 film, *Santa Sangre*.

*Santa Sangre* has been described as a horror film and a glorious return to your panic roots. But it was also your first attempt to turn and see your tail, and when you did, it was bloody and gory and violent as fuck. The wound was tender, too tender to address directly. So, the murderer Goyo Cardenas stood in for you during the film, giving you the artistic space to kill and bury as many people as it took to free your hands from your mother's control. In this way, *Santa Sangre* was also a poetic act.

I am also grateful for the stories of your earliest childhood poetic acts detailed in your book *Psychomagic: The Transformative Power of Shamanic Psychotherapy*. I particularly enjoyed the story in which you covered your money-obsessed father with worms while he slept to remind him of his mortality. It is tragic that these acts never resulted in a bond between the two of you. But it is beautiful that even though he is gone, you still created an entire film, 2013's *La Danza de la Realidad*, your first film in 23 years, as an act of psychomagic to heal your father's ailment.

The wounds our fathers can inflict upon us are like derelict houses we inherit long before they are dead. Then, it is our job to fix it or be doomed to re-inflict similar or opposite trauma upon our children. You know this as well as I do. I repeat it to you because this is a game of telephone. And in this life, what is not a game? You were conceived by an act of your father's violence, by the rape of your mother. It is a wildly poetic universe indeed that would send the seed of your father's iniquity to heal his bloodline.

And thus, we arrive at the end of our story. Alejandro, I have spared much space for your adventures to continue. I feel that there is so much more to tell. And I would love to write it, but first, I need you to create another 80 years' worth of art.

*"I promised you the great secret, and I will not disappoint you. Is this the end of our adventure? Nothing has an end. We came in search of the secret of immortality, to be like gods. And here we are, mortals, more human than ever. If we have not obtained immortality, at least we have obtained reality. We began in a fairytale, and we came to life."*

*-The Holy Mountain*

# Epilogue

After a few months, once everyone had had their laughs, and the king's novelty died down, then Alejandro came to visit his father. As he approached, children scattered, laughing. Alejandro's appearance had gained a new, unnerving attribute from his prolonged exposure to powerful magic; sometimes, he appeared very young, while other times, very old.

The king wore a pink and white bonnet of spring flowers the children had placed atop his head. "Children, they are precious, no?" Alejandro chuckled a little. "Listen, and I will tell you a great secret. It is true what mothers say: they are each built uniquely. But they are not their own. They are little energy converters, part of the great lungs of the universe. They will grow to blame themselves for their perceived failures, not knowing they are like the tide pulled by the moon. And thus, it must be—for now.

The ass bleated such a line of obscenities that even Alejandro could not decipher their meaning.

"Do not be upset, father. Take heart. How many mortals get to live more than one life without dying? And, don't worry; eventually, I will turn you into something— something else, dependent on what you must learn. I will heal you, father. I must if I am to alter my cycle."

The donkey cocked his head to one side, and Alejandro laughed. "You are curious! Good! We will have many adventures. We will sail to the land beyond the god's control. And then, then, I will just have to dream up something else."

# About Atmosphere Press

Atmosphere Press is an independent, full-service publisher for excellent books in all genres and for all audiences. Learn more about what we do at atmospherepress.com.

We encourage you to check out some of Atmosphere's latest releases, which are available at Amazon.com and via order from your local bookstore:

*Tales of Little Egypt,* a historical novel by James Gilbert
*For a Better Life,* a novel by Julia Reid Galosy
*The Hidden Life,* a novel by Robert Castle
*Big Beasts,* a novel by Patrick Scott
*Alvarado,* a novel by John W. Horton III
*Nothing to Get Nostalgic About*, a novel by Eddie Brophy
*GROW: A Jack and Lake Creek Book,* a novel by Chris S McGee
*Home is Not This Body,* a novel by Karahn Washington
*Whose Mary Kate,* a novel by Jane Leclere Doyle
*Stuck and Drunk in Shadyside,* young adult fiction by M. Byerly
*These Things Happen,* a novel by Chris Caldwell
*Vanity: Murder in the Name of Sin,* a novel by Rhiannon Garrard
*Blood of the True Believer,* a novel by Brandann R. Hill-Mann

# About the Author

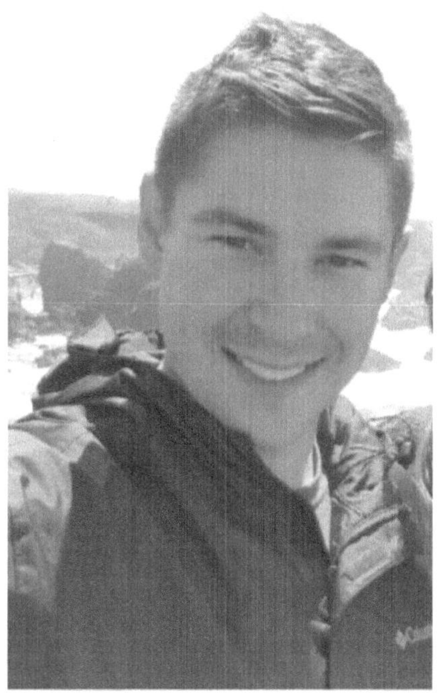

Nathan Dean Talamantez is a Bay Area transplant from Texas, Air Force veteran, and current student pursuant of his MFA from California Institute of Integral studies. Dean received his undergraduate in cultural anthropology in 2013 from Texas State University. His writing tends toward the examination of complex social issues from unfamiliar and often surreal angles.